# DESCRIPTION

*Embark on a transformative journey to a calmer and more fulfilling life with this comprehensive guide on meditation and mindfulness.*

*This self-help book equips you with scientifically-backed tools to manage stress, anxiety, and negative thoughts. Discover the power of mindfulness in rewiring your brain and fostering positive thinking. Incorporate lifestyle changes, such as minimalism and health-focused habits, to complement your meditation practice. Ideal for beginners and seasoned practitioners, this book is your roadmap to a happier, healthier, and calmer state of mind.*

*Start your life-changing journey today!*

# DISCLAIMER

*This book has been written for information purposes only. Every effort has been made to make this information as complete and accurate as possible. However, there may be mistakes in typography or content. Also, this book provides information only up to the publishing date. Therefore, this book should be used as a guide - not as the ultimate source.*

*The purpose of this book is to educate. The author and the publisher do not warrant that the information contained in this book is fully complete and shall not be responsible for any errors or omissions. The author and publisher shall have neither liability nor responsibility to any person or entity concerning any loss or damage caused or alleged to be caused directly or indirectly by this book.*

# TABLE OF CONTENTS

# INTRODUCTION 06

# CHAPTERS

01: **Why You Are Always Stressed – And Why it Needs to Stop** 10
Where Does Stress Come From?
The Function of Stress

02: **Just What is Meditation?** 16
Types of Meditation
Making Sense of It All

03: **How to Get Started With Meditation** 28

04: **Just What is Mindfulness?** 36
The Role of Mindfulness

05: **Cognitive Behavioral Therapy**    40
     **Explained**
     Mindfulness and CBT
     Mindful Washing Up

06: **Using Cognitive Restructuring**    46
     **to Become Calmer and Happier**
     How to Combat Anxiety With CBT

07: **Understanding Stress,**    49
     **Meditation, and Your Brain**
     Your Brain on Stress VS Meditation

08: **Optimizing Your Life, Diet,**    54
     **and Habits for Less Stress and**
     **Greater Fulfillment**
     Minimalism
     Unplugging
     Health

# CONCLUSION    62

INTRODUCTION

# INTRODUCTION

Meditation can completely change your life. While countless products, remedies, hacks, and lifestyle changes all promise to hold the 'answer,' only meditation comes close to delivering on that promise. And this is no coincidence: it's simply because meditation is the only method among these that focuses on helping you to improve yourself. Through meditation, you dig deep and change how you approach life and situations. It gives you more command over your mind and will, and helps you to become the best version of yourself.

Meditation helps you to rise above stress and worry, thereby finding peace in your every day – and improving your happiness, health, and general well-being to a huge degree. Moreover, though, meditation can also help to improve your performance by bringing stress under control. It can help you to focus your attention like a laser, become unflappable in a crisis, and tap into reserves of creativity, compassion, and wisdom that you never knew you had.

The problem is that meditation is too often thought of as this 'mystical' practice, with strong ties to religion, spirituality, and even mysticism. Many people will therefore be put off before they even start. Others might recognize the growing acceptance of meditation as a proven, scientific method for encouraging positive changes in the brain at a biological level – but still find themselves daunted.

How do you begin to start? How can you calm a mind that doesn't want to be still? How can you possibly find the time?

This book is going to explore all of those things and more. Throughout this time, you will discover the significant types of meditation, how they are different, and how to use them. What's more, is that you will learn how to employ those forms of meditation in a manner that is practical, easy, and highly effective.

We will be demystifying what should be a very simple and powerful tool. By the end, the power will be in your hands to take the core principles of meditation and mindfulness and apply them in a manner meaningful to your life.

## INTRODUCTION

*In this book, you will learn:*

- Where stress comes from and why you need to deal with it
- The different types of meditation and what they are each for
- How to start meditation in an easy and convenient way
- How to progress and improve in your meditation practice
- How to use mindfulness in everyday life
- How to use metacognition to understand yovur thoughts
- How to overcome anxiety and stress with CBT and cognitive restructuring
- How meditation affects the brain
- How to improve your lifestyle for even greater calm

# WHY YOU ARE ALWAYS STRESSED — AND WHY IT NEEDS TO STOP

CHAPTER 01

Many of us are unaware of just how severe a problem stress is. We live in a semi-permanent state of anxiety and arousal, but the most shocking part is that we act as if this is okay – expected even. After all, everyone else we know is stressed too, so how can it be a big problem? However, stress is a very serious problem that will not only prevent you from fully enjoying your life in the short term – but may make you seriously ill over time.

**WHERE DOES STRESS COME FROM?**

You don't need to look hard to find where all this stress comes from in our modern lives. Anything that causes stress is what we call a 'stressor,' and these are all around us all the time. Some are physical, while others are mental.

Consider how you start your day: by being woken up with a start in the pitch black, by a bleeping noise. Did you know that we chose beeping alarms because it sounds unnatural? That means that the brain fires up on red alert, and sends panic signals by releasing cortisol and adrenaline into your body. You've only just woken up, and you're already probably suffering from whiplash!

Then you rush to get ready, heart racing as you worry about what happens if you're late – and perhaps dread whatever stressful thing you must handle that day in the office.

Then you head off on your commute, people pushing past you and walking toward you. Horns blaring, smoke thick in the air, and bright billboards flashing in your eyes. All these things, vying for your attention and triggering more spikes in excitatory neurotransmitters.

At work, you undoubtedly need to deal with office politics, deadlines, and people shouting at you down the phone… with the potential prospect of losing your job if you don't do well, always looming over you. The unnatural light you're bathed in meanwhile triggers even more arousal, with none of the nourishing effects of vitamin D and fresh air.

Or maybe you're a stay-at-home parent? In which case, your day will revolve around responding to the screams and cries of your child, struggling to keep the house tidy, and in the time in between, making food in a hot kitchen, worrying about bills…

Meanwhile, most activities we engage in when we try to 'relax' involve looking at flashing lights and images of people fighting. When we flick through magazines, we find ourselves constantly pressured to look better, perform better, and spend more money.

Even Facebook is filled with people projecting a false image of success – one that we feel pressured to live up to.

## THE FUNCTION OF STRESS

The purpose of stress is to put our body in a state of high

alert. This is what we know as the 'fight or flight response.' This should be a response to immediate danger that thereby helps to improve our chances of survival in a fight or when fleeing from a fire. Thus, our breathing increases, our body produces more adrenaline and cortisol, our heart rate goes up, our blood viscosity increases to prevent us from bleeding out, our pupils dilate to let in more light, and our brain activity goes through the roof thinking of all the possible dangers around us. During this, our blood vessels dilate and restrict to control the flow of blood – away from the organs and digestive system, and toward the muscles and brain. This is similar to when the captain of a spaceship in a TV series says,

"Reroute all power to thrusters!"

"Even the med bay, sir?"

"Even the med bay."

In other words, while your physical and mental performance technically increases, all secondary functions are on the back burner. You don't need them right now. And in the short term, this is fine. However, in the long term, chronic stress can ultimately be crippling as it suppresses the activity of the digestive system, thereby preventing us from properly absorbing nutrients and suppressing the immune system –

leaving us open to attack from germs.

Stress makes us constantly think of the worst-case scenarios, so it becomes self-perpetuating. We are stressed about money, and so we become even more stressed about money. We get into arguments with our loved ones. We place strain on our relationships. Our panic leads us to make silly mistakes which put us in further trouble. We bury our heads in the sand and ignore important jobs like answering letters and paying bills.

It's a lifestyle that is ultimately unsustainable, and that is certainly not rewarding or fulfilling. And that's where meditation comes in – as THE most effective way to get your head back above water, and your life back on track.

# JUST WHAT IS MEDITATION?

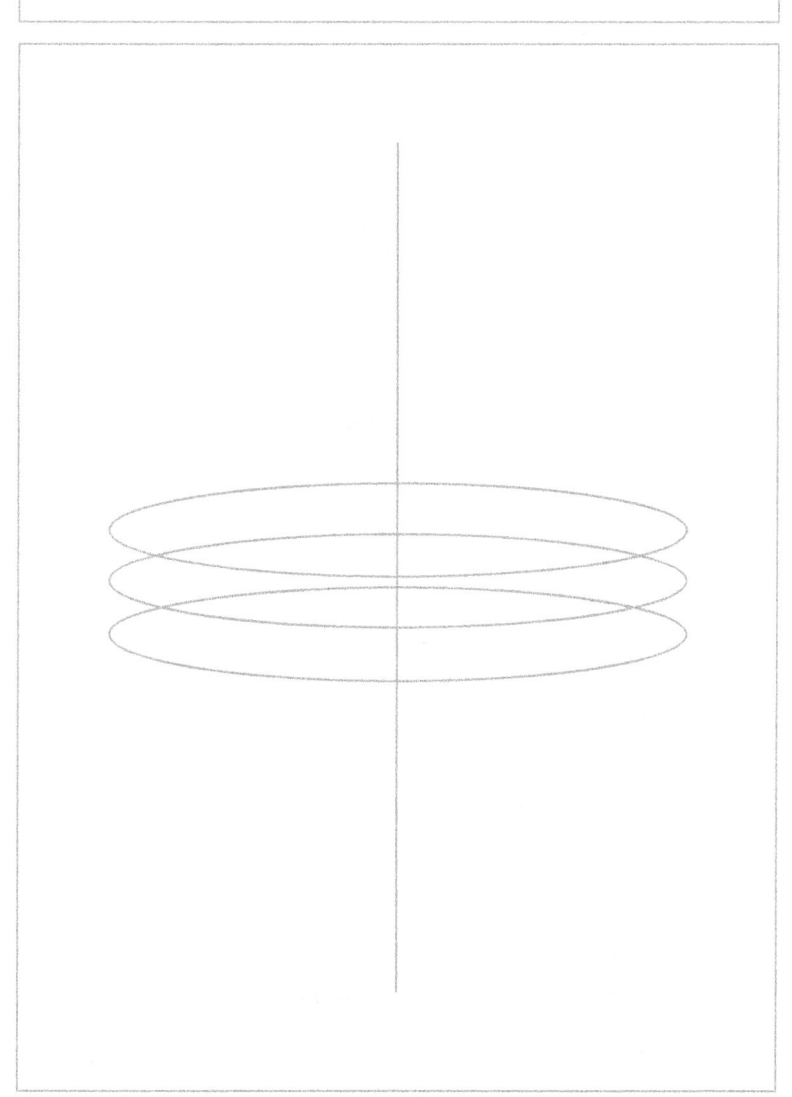

CHAPTER 02

We all have a notion of what meditation is. Most of us picture someone sitting in the lotus position, with their hands balanced delicately on their knees, repeating the sound 'Om' over and over.

This is not incorrect, nor is it a particularly detailed or helpful picture of what's going on. But perhaps asking 'what is meditation' is the wrong question. After all, there are many different types of mediation, each of which utilizes slightly different methods, and has slightly different goals and aims. With that said, they also still have a lot in common. Let's start by taking a look at each, and then see what we can take from all of them at the end.

## TYPES OF MEDITATION:

### Transcendental Meditation

One of the most popular and well-known forms of meditation, by far, is transcendental meditation – or TM. This type of meditation originally comes from India during the 1950s and is practiced by many high-profile celebrities. The general concept, however, is very simple and is one of the most tested. Simply, practitioners are tasked with completely emptying their minds of all thoughts and all distractions. They do this by focusing on something – which will very often be a mantra. A mantra is just a word or phrase that you repeat over and over, and this could be as simple as the word 'Om' (so that's where that comes from!). The mantra should have no meaning because the aim is not to 'reflect' on meaning and thereby trap yourself at the 'surface level.'

The aim is to focus on this mantra, and then allow all other distractions to sink away. If you notice yourself thinking about something else, just calmly bring your mind back to the point of focus and calm.

Transcendental meditation is a regulated form of meditation that is led by instructors. However, it is also very similar in aim and method to other forms, such as Vedic meditation. We can use TM as a broad term to describe almost any form of meditation where the objective is to empty the mind by focusing on a singular quale (stimulus).

### Loving Kindness Meditation

Loving-kindness meditation is a form of meditation that involves focusing your attention entirely on feelings and thoughts of kindness and love. These can be directed toward others, but they can also be directed toward yourself. That means that you're going to be cultivating these feelings – enjoying the warm bask of kind feelings at times when you're feeling low or stressed, but ultimately reinforcing these habits so that you become more likely to fall back on those kinds of feelings, rather than sinking into negativity and doubt quickly.

This is a form of Buddhist meditation and is best learned with the help of a teacher – though, of course, it is possible to practice it very similarly on your own.

**Body Scan/Progressive Relaxation**
Body scan meditation is often used in conjunction with mindfulness meditation and is what we can think of as a form of 'kinesthetic meditation' (meaning that the focus is on the body and the way you feel).

This kind of meditation aims to gradually move your focus across your body while relaxing each muscle during the process. Throughout the day, we all carry a lot of muscle tension.
Some of this is caused by stress, some by knots in the fascia that surround your muscle, and some by normal, healthy tension known as 'tonus' (this is what helps to keep a slight tautness in the muscles and prevents our body from completely relaxing in a limp heap!).

When you use progressive relaxation, you aim to release as much of this tension as possible – calming the mind as a byproduct. So, you might start by focusing on your forehead. Is there any tension in your brow? How about your ears? Contract each muscle, then make a conscious effort to release it – breathing out slowly as you do to ensure that the area is fully relaxed.

This form of meditation not only distracts you from your troubles and helps you to get 'out of your head,' but also gives you the ability to fully relax on cue. This can be a beneficial method for getting to sleep, for example, if you struggle with insomnia.

### Breath Awareness Meditation

Breath awareness meditation is exactly what it sounds like a form of meditation that involves focusing your full attention on the breath. This can mean counting your breaths, breathing in a specific manner (later in this book, we'll talk about yogic belly breathing), or simply focusing on your breath.

Whatever the case, this once again provides you with a single focal point, and the idea is to release all other thoughts so that your mind becomes quiet and calm.

### Gazing Meditation

Gazing meditation is a yogic tradition that is 'externally focused.' All that means is that you will be focusing on something outside of your own body – which might mean that you're focusing on the movement of a flame, a running river, or something else entirely.

If your eyes become tired or you need to blink, close your eyes and try to focus on the afterimage of what you were gazing at. Then, when ready, open them slowly again. This can again be used in the same way as TM – the idea is to calm the mind and remove distracting and unhelpful thoughts.

Many people find this to be one of the more straightforward methods to get started with, as there is a useful outside distraction. Try to think back to the last time that you found yourself gazing off into the distance, having wholly lost yourself – that is the state of mind you're trying to get to. Knowing this is your goal, it can make it easier to return to again. Kundalini Yoga Meditation Kundalini yoga meditation is a form of meditation that incorporates specific movements, diet, and more. The aim is that you're going to be looking to improve your flexibility, muscle tone, and strength, while at the same time calming the mind and improving your breathing – getting a whole lot of bang for your buck.

Furthermore, breathing is performed slightly differently in kundalini meditation. Here, you block the left nostril and use a prolonged, deep inhalation. Next, you block the right nostril, and as you do this, you allow the mind to clear.

**Nada Meditation**
Nada meditation is another yogic method that involves using an outside stimulus. This time though, you will be focusing on another sense: hearing.

Nada meditation means focusing on one sound, which can mean listening to the sound of a nearby running stream and the singing birds, or even the sounds of cars and traffic if you live in a city. You can alternatively open yourself up to all the sounds around you and take a moment to stop and listen to as many sounds as possible. It might surprise you to learn just how many sounds you miss out on normally – and how much you can hear when you broaden your scope.

Nada meditation can also be achieved using music, which many people find is an easy way to get themselves lost without thought.

### Vedic Meditation

Vedic meditation is extremely similar to transcendental meditation but without branding and marketing. Essentially, it involves focusing on a mantra to calm the mind and body. There is little functional difference between these two forms of meditation, but seek out TM if you need an instructor and guidance.

### Zazen Meditation

Zazen Meditation is a form of Buddhist meditation. Like TM, it requires an instructor to get the real deal, but in practice, it is incredibly similar to mindfulness meditation – which we will explore in much greater depth later. The aim is essentially to try and detach from the thoughts and to allow them to go past 'without judgment.'

You are not emptying the mind, simply disengaging from it.

### Chi Kung

From Shaolin Kung Fu, Chi Kung is a form of meditation that means 'energy work'. Its objective is to help practitioners visualize the flow of 'chi' (qi) around the body, to enhance health and strength Of course, your belief in chi may vary – but whatever your interpretation, the visualization can help you to better focus the mind and even develop a better connection to your own body.

Chi Kung involves holding several positions, which place a light amount of strain on the body. This further helps to route the mind in the body, as does gently moving occasionally from one to the other. You will practice controlled breathing, and at the same time, bring the mind to the center – or the 'dan tien' – which is located a couple of centimeters below the navel and also happens to be the center of gravity.

### Tai Chi

Tai Chi is a form of meditation closely linked to Chi Kung. Here, the movement is far more continuous, with practitioners gently progressing through stances and movements. Again, the idea is to use this as a form of kinesthetic meditation, wherein the focus on the body helps to clear the mind. At the same time, though, this can also be an excellent way to develop greater control over the body and greater strength. Each of these movements has a martial application, and when delivered with speed and power, can be deadly.

### Third Eye Meditation

Whereas chi kung focuses the attention on the dantian (just below the navel), this form of meditation involves focusing on the point in the middle of your forehead, just above and between the eyes.

### Religious Meditation

Christian meditation is a form of meditation that – of course – is practiced by Christians. It involves focusing on a passage from the bible or a prayer and reflecting on its meaning and any attached emotion. But this method can, of course, be used by practitioners of any faith, providing a valuable way for them to combine their religion with the health benefits of meditation.

Of course, you could just as quickly focus on something else: how about thinking about the film you just saw? What about a poem that you respond to deeply?

### Self-Enquiry Meditation

For those who want their meditation to be a bit more spiritual but perhaps don't want to adhere to any particular religion, self-inquiry is an ideal form of meditation. Here, you focus on yourself, your beliefs, and your goals. Where do you see yourself heading in life? What is the meaning of your existence? Are you happy? This is another form of yogic meditation, and of course, has a lot of potentially profound benefits.

### Productive Meditation

Productive meditation is distinctly not spiritual and seems almost an anathema to meditation – though this is not true, as we will see in a moment. You see, productive meditation – first suggested by Cal Newport in the book Deep Work – is a type of meditation focused on a problem in your work or personal life. Or perhaps you're trying to think of something creative. Maybe you're trying to come up with a new idea.

### Mindfulness Meditation

Mindfulness meditation is the last item on this list, not because it is obscure because it is perhaps the most popular option right now – but because we're about to dive into it in much more detail. This has recently become famous thanks to the prevalence of CBT (cognitive behavioral therapy) in psychotherapeutic schools, which involves detaching yourself from your thought.

You do this by deciding to 'sit back' and 'watch' your thoughts go by. Often the analogy is given that you are 'watching clouds move across the sky.' So, you don't tell yourself off for thinking something, and nor do you force a thought. You just let them pass, and you consciously try to be aware of them as they do.

## MAKING SENSE OF IT ALL

You got this book to understand meditation and hopefully start incorporating it into your life and enjoying its benefits. But perhaps you're now reading this and feeling overwhelmed and confused. With so many different kinds of meditation to try, how can you possibly know what the best type is for you? And if there are so many kinds, how can they all be called the same thing?

Well, if we look at all these forms of meditation logically, we can see that they have a lot in common. Despite their differences, they are all examples of employing focus. You might be focusing on your breathing, you might be focusing on your muscle. You might be focusing on a candle flame or a babbling brook. You might be focusing on a passage of religious text or an idea. But in each case, you are focusing. And that's really what the mind needs. In the 21st century, we have all become far too distractable. Everything is vying for our attention, from those billboards we talked about to the beeps from your phone, to your boss and partner.

All this means that we have very little say over what we think about and when, and we have become bad at deciding just to sit down and focus for a while. And when we do try to, we have somewhat lost the method. That, in turn, means that when we are worried, or when we are sad, we have lost the ability to not think about it. When spending time with friends and loved ones, we may struggle likewise to listen to what they're saying and have fun – rather than thinking about global warming or our bank accounts.

That's how meditation helps you to feel calmer and happier – it becomes a place that you can 'go to' at any point to escape all the other thoughts. In doing so, the heart rate slows, the blood cools, and you feel better. Moreover, learning to focus attention helps you to be more productive when you need to be. To be more creative. To perform better in sports – even in the bedroom. By choosing how to control your attention and what to attend to, you become a master of your mood – and this puts you back in control.

We'll go over more of the benefits of meditation in a subsequent chapter, but for now, that's what you need to know. Now let's get started, shall we?

# HOW TO GET STARTED WITH MEDITATION

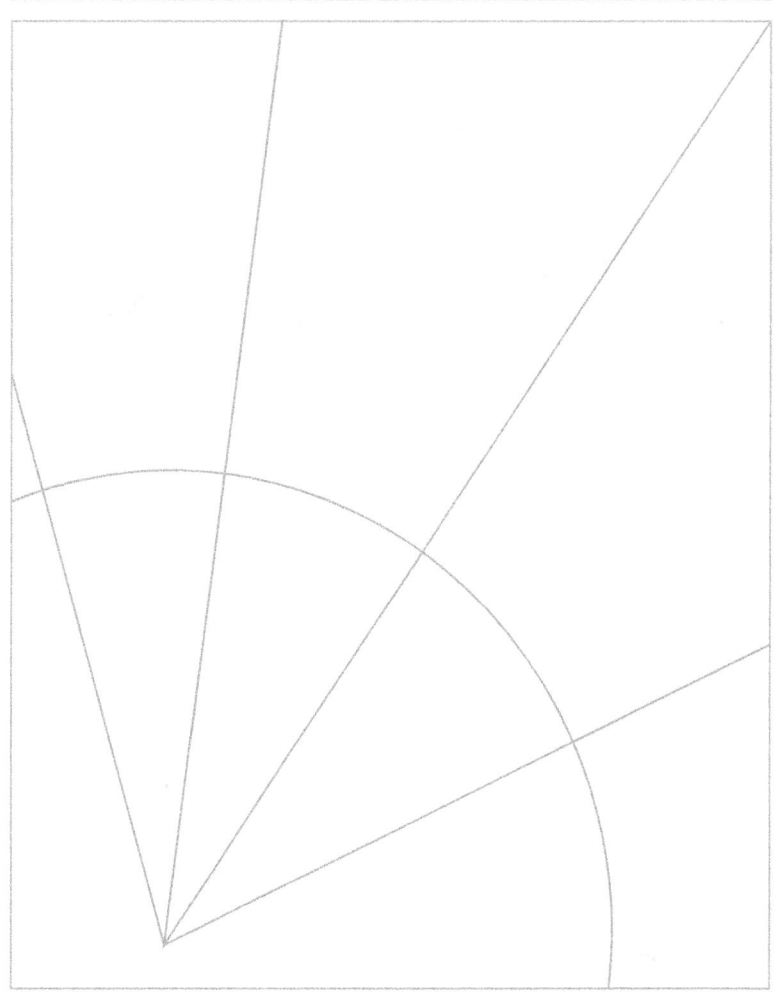

CHAPTER 03

Now you know what meditation is, and you know about all the different types available, it's time to give it a go.
This is where most people fall, but you're not most people… are you?

The problem that many people find is that they place too much pressure on themselves to be perfect immediately. They are too strict with their approach, and they worry about not having the time. Ultimately, this becomes just another thing they need to do, another thing they're not doing well enough… just another source of stress! And as you might imagine, that's not what we're aiming for here. So how do you get started with meditation?

**STEP 1 – PICK A STYLE**

We've just gone over the many different types of meditation, so now it's time to think about the one with the most significant appeal to you. You don't need to be wed to it forever! Choose the one that you think you might enjoy, and if it doesn't work out, you can always try something different next time.

Good ones to start with for beginners are:

- Nada Meditation
- Mindfulness
- Breath Awareness
- TM/Vedic
- Body Scan

Another option is to try using guided meditation. There are plenty of these on YouTube (just search guided [INSERT TYPE] meditation), and you can also find apps like Headspace (www.headspace.com). Headspace uses mindfulness and is not free, but it is well made, and the first ten sessions are available without signing up – so there's no reason not to try it.

One question many people have is whether they can combine more than one type of meditation. The answer to this is: absolutely! Remember: the real benefit you are getting from meditation is that it is going to help you feel a sense of calm and to build your focus. With the overall target being the same, you can liken switching between meditation styles to combining press-ups and bench pressing into a single workout. Not only is it possible, but it will also help you to get a better end result. But for simplicity, try to stick with one form of meditation, so you don't get overwhelmed.

## STEP 2 – FIND A COMFORTABLE SPACE

Where and when should you meditate? As we will see later, the answer is 'anywhere, anytime.' For now, though, you might want to start with a comfortable space that is quiet and free from distractions. Being able to meditate in a crowded coffee shop is a skill in itself but not ideal for beginners. What's more is that it can be potentially dangerous, seeing as you will be unaware of your surroundings. Likewise, the mere thought that your peace might be suddenly interrupted can be enough to prevent you from getting into a calm state of mind. If you are using a seated form of meditation, find a comfortable surface where you can sit cross-legged, on your knees, in the lotus position, or otherwise. A chair will do just fine, but your back must be straight to encourage proper breathing (more on this in a future chapter).

However, you will want to avoid lying down, as this will make it too easy to fall asleep – while beneficial, sleep is not the same as meditation! You can do whatever you like with your hands, but many people find it easiest to place them gently on their legs or knees.

## STEP 3 – SET SOME TIME

You should now set a defined amount of time. And this is where the next question arises: what is the ideal amount of time to meditate? What is the minimum?

Once more, the answer to this question is very fluid. If you speak with a long-time practitioner of Vedic meditation, they might tell you to try meditating for 20 minutes twice a day. Indeed, something like this might have a profound effect on your state of mind and your health.

While this is true, it's also more than many people can commit to. If you attempt to meditate for this large amount of time, you may well find that you simply end up quitting and then feeling stressed that you aren't making the progress you hoped to see by that stage.

So, just setting a timer for five minutes is an excellent way to begin experimenting with meditation, and this will still have a lot of beneficial effects. How you do this is up to you, but setting a timer on a phone (making sure to choose a non-startling tone!) is an excellent way to give yourself a kind of 'protected' bubble of time where you know you won't be interrupted. The bubble allows you to completely relax, knowing that you aren't going to be interrupted and aren't going to accidentally run over into the time you need for productive tasks. Even five minutes twice a week is fine. But if you can spare the time, aim for 10 minutes a day, or half an hour twice a week for a happy compromise.

**Some More Tips**: If your eyes will be open, then what you stare at will have an important bearing on how you feel. If you sit in an untidy room, this can cause a little bit of anxiety and prevent you from properly relaxing. Tidy your space if possible, and better yet: try keeping a room that is emptier and dedicated to meditation.

Another option is to head outside. Being immersed in nature is extremely good for your mental health, and this gives you lots of calming options for how to focus. If you have a well-tended garden, then this will do the trick. Otherwise, perhaps there is a favorite spot nearby you could try? You could also find a relaxing place while traveling on holiday. There's nothing quite like taking a moment to sit atop a mountain and drink in a beautiful waterfall (not literally).

**Note**: Of course, for meditation forms that involve standing or moving, you might need to go somewhere else. Many people practice Tai Chi in parks or at the beach, for example. When practicing body scan meditation, ensure your back is supported, or you are lying flat – otherwise, you risk collapsing!

## STEP 4 – SIT QUIETLY

Now it's time to direct your attention to whatever it is you will focus on during the meditation. That might be the passage of text, your mental state, music, a candle, or your body. Your objective is to stop your mind from wandering. It is perfectly natural for you to find yourself thinking things like:

'Did I leave the stove on?'

Or

'My colleague was unpleasant to me at work yesterday.'

You might also find yourself thinking about your attempt to meditate! Common are thoughts like:

'Wow, thoughts keep entering my mind!'

Or

'I am not doing really well at meditating.'

Don't worry if this happens – just like any form of exercise or any new skill, meditation takes practice. So, when you notice that your mind has wandered, all you need to do is to bring your thoughts gently back to the point of focus.

Don't punish yourself for giving up, and don't worry if you need to scratch your face. The less you allow these things to bother you, the more effortless meditation will be. Don't run before you can walk: if you only manage five minutes of sitting relatively quietly, that is still remarkable progress.

# JUST WHAT IS MINDFULNESS?

CHAPTER 04

So now you have a good understanding of meditation and the knowledge you need to start it. You can pick a form of meditation from the list in chapter two, start practicing it, and enjoy reaping the benefits. But if you want to take this transformation to the next level, then you might also think about incorporating mindfulness. We've danced around this topic a little so far, now it's time to dive right in.

## THE ROLE OF MINDFULNESS

If you want to change your life for the better, then the answer most likely does not lie with changing things around you. This is the first mistake that many of us tend to make: we think that we are unhappy because we don't have enough stuff, or because we aren't successful enough. Maybe we blame our partners, our health, and our looks. But guess what: none of those things will make you happy and fulfilled.

This isn't just an empty platitude either: it's a scientific fact, based on research. The truth is that even substantial life changes don't alter our mood that much. In one famous study, researchers will use tests to measure the happiness of participants immediately after winning the lottery and immediately after losing a limb. As you can imagine, the first group is typically much happier. But then the researchers will follow up with the same test, conducted again years later. And this time, they find that both groups have settled and have roughly equal happiness. This is what psychologists and sociologists refer to as the 'hedonistic treadmill.' The notion is that there is a kind of baseline of 'minor dissatisfaction' that is normal for humans. We always return to this state, because that is what our evolutionary history has mandated.

It doesn't make any sense to be miserable to the point of being frozen – that won't help your survival. But likewise, it also doesn't make sense to be extremely happy. If you were extremely happy and content all the time, then what would be the point in chasing after goals, or improving your situation at all? It is our slight dissatisfaction that has motivated mankind throughout the ages to achieve so much and to grow and develop. In short, that 'itch' is hardwired into us; it is an evolutionary legacy.

So how can you ever be happy? Well, several schools of thought have identified that the key to happiness, in this case, is not to change the things in your life but rather to change how you think about those things. Change the way you appreciate them. This is the concept behind stoicism, for instance, which teaches that we should stop trying to make a perfect world and instead become better at accepting the world we are presented with. And it's also true of mindfulness, though in this case, it's a little more positive.

How can changing the way you view a situation change how happy you are? It's a little like being the 'half glass full' kind of person, and simply choosing to see the good in any situation. To put it another way: imagine that you're in a beautiful, natural location. There's a babbling stream nearby, a cool breeze, and an amazing array of mountains and waterfalls in the distance. You'd be pretty calm, am I right? But, what if a lion was waiting in the bush just nearby? Suddenly, that same situation becomes far more sinister and far less relaxing. In short, that 'itch' is hard-wired into us, it is an evolutionary legacy.

The problem is when you imagine lions that aren't there. And we do this all the time. And when that possibility of a lion is all you can think about, it's something that can prevent you from being happy. The idea of mindfulness, then, is to become aware of what you're thinking, and then choose what you will focus on and how you will operate.

# COGNITIVE BEHAVIORAL THERAPY EXPLAINED

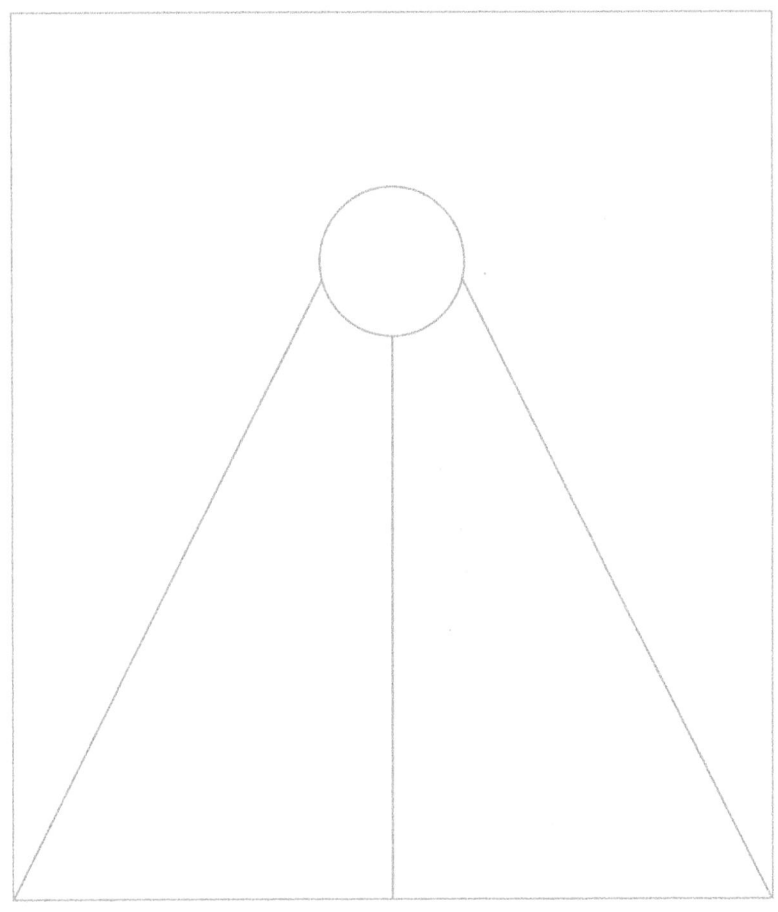

CHAPTER 05

The problem is that most of us never even think to take control of our thoughts. The rest struggle to accomplish that goal, even if they do try. Therefore, we remain reactive: reacting to everything that happens and letting that control our emotions. Focusing on all the wrong things, panicking about things that really shouldn't matter to us. You might find yourself dreaming of owning things that you can't afford, instead of appreciating the things you have and should be thankful for.

Mindfulness helps us think positively and efficiently, instead of reactively and in a stressed and charged manner.

### A Mindfulness Challenge

To demonstrate just how little most of us can control our thoughts or our attention, you could try this mindfulness challenge.

What you're going to do, is to try and count how many times you sit down during the day. Every time you go to sit down, remember to count that sitting action. This might sound like the easiest challenge in the world, but the hard bit is that you often won't remember to do it. If you manage to count more than one of these (getting up and sitting down again right now doesn't count!), you can consider yourself very 'in the moment' and doing well. This might initially shock you, but it shows just how distracted most of us are.

## MINDFULNESS AND CBT

Mindfulness, used in this way, often goes hand-in-hand with CBT. So just what is CBT? Essentially, CBT is an attempt to become more aware of your thoughts, and then to take back control of them. That's precisely what we do when we choose to count the number of times we sit up and stand up, but it can also be what we do when we choose to use a 'gratitude attitude' instead of focusing on the things we don't have, or can't have.

So, CBT stands for 'Cognitive Behavioral Therapy,' and the way you might use it includes:

- Practice using mindfulness meditation. Remember, this means simply watching your thoughts go by so that you are aware of what you're thinking at that moment. Try not to judge the content of those thoughts, try to control them, or feel bad about them. Just dispassionately watch them.

- Eventually, you should try to start making notes of the kinds of things you are thinking during the day too. This is also called 'metacognition' or thinking about thinking. Ask yourself:

    » How does this make me feel? Why?
    » Did I react to that well?

- » Should I be stressed about the thing I've been worrying about?
- » How am I feeling right now?

- Try to take conscious control of what you're thinking. Make sure to enjoy time with your family by being 'present.' Try to leave your problems at work. Try to focus fully when being creative or productive, etc.

- Keep a journal; use this journal to write down the kinds of thoughts you might have, and to try and replace them with things you'd rather be thinking.

- Consider employing the 'gratitude attitude' by making lists of what you are thankful for, or writing three things you appreciated at the end of every day. Doing this will help you to focus on the good instead of the bad.

- Try to replace some of your negative thoughts with positive mantras. Unlike the mantras used in Vedic meditation, these should have meaning and are designed to help you replace negative thoughts and build more positive patterns. For example:

  - » It doesn't matter what people think
  - » I have plenty of things I want already
  - » I have a family that loves me

» I am skilled and capable

If you practice these things, you may eventually find that you stop being so upset by things that would typically get to you.

## MINDFUL WASHING UP

Mindfulness then can be as simple as choosing to focus on something and thereby turning a mundane activity into a form of meditation. An excellent example of this is a popular trend called 'mindful washing up.' The simple concept is you are going to turn an everyday activity (washing up in this case), into something that can be practiced as a form of meditation. So, as you are washing up, focus on it 100%. Try to make it a repetitive action and just watch the bubbles and feel the sponge.

If you can do this, you can turn anything into meditation – from walking to jogging, from reading to looking out the window for five minutes. Suddenly, you find moments of calm in everything you do, and you start to see and experience the world again.

# USING COGNITIVE RESTRUCTURING TO BECOME CALMER AND HAPPIER

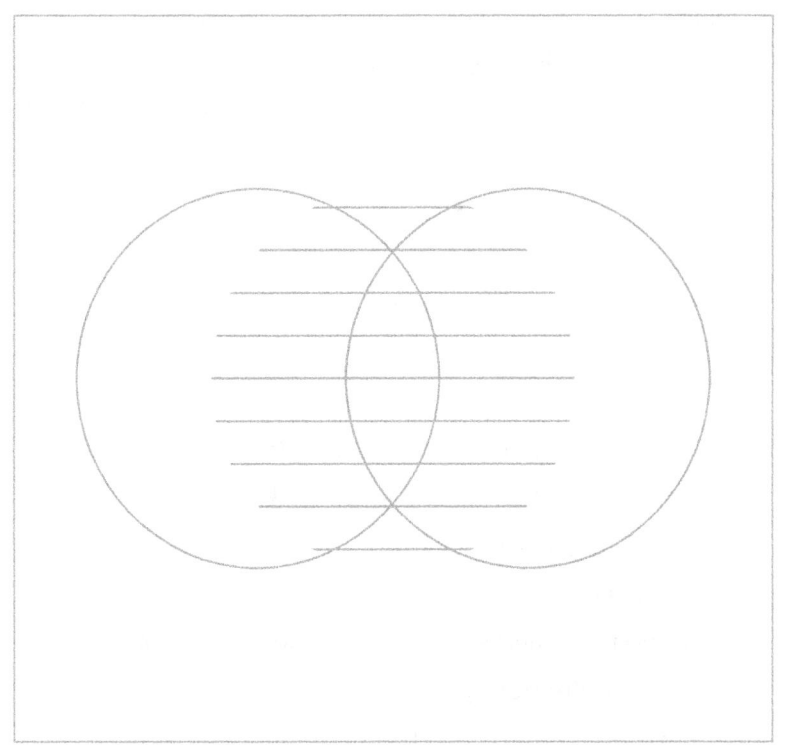

CHAPTER 06

The next step in cognitive restructuring is really interesting, though. While it doesn't directly relate to meditation on its own, we'll touch on it here as it is somewhat relevant. The idea behind cognitive restructuring is mastering the ability to be aware of your thoughts, you are now going to start 'restructuring them' to become more positive. We have already done that to an extent, by choosing to focus on positives, by using mantras, and by being thankful. But now we're going to begin the process of systematically dismantling negative beliefs. You can use this to destroy social anxiety, overcome insomnia, defeat phobias, and more.

## HOW TO COMBAT ANXIETY WITH CBT

So, let's say, for instance, that you have a social phobia. You're going to start now by using metacognition and perhaps mindfulness meditation the next time that you're feeling stressed about a social event. What is it specifically that you are afraid of? What are you thinking about right now that is making you anxious?

Often, you might find that you feel scared you'll say the wrong thing, and someone will laugh at you. Maybe you think you're going to offend someone or do something wrong. Perhaps you think you're going to stutter. Whatever the case, there is likely a 'worst-case scenario' that you're picturing.

Now you can use two cognitive restructuring techniques to dismantle that image. These are:

- Thought challenging
- Hypothesis testing

Thought challenging means that you will actively assess your concern for validity. Just how accurate is this? How likely is it that your fear will become a reality? In the case of 'saying the wrong thing and everyone laughing at you,' you are likely to find that this is not likely, for example. That's because most people aren't so unkind as to laugh when you make a mistake. Who are these people? Your friends? Most people are just as nervous as you, and if you stutter or make a mistake, they'll probably smile and wait for you to correct yourself.

Likewise, how likely are you to blurt out something stupid? If you're this concerned, you'll probably watch what you're saying. Just pause a little before talking, and you should be fine. And anyway, what does it matter if they do laugh? Can't you just laugh at yourself with them? If they are laughing in a mean-spirited manner, then is this truly someone you want to impress/spend time with anyway? Assess this logically, and if you believe that your thought is unfounded by the end – then you should find that it loses its power over you.

The next step is hypothesis testing, which is a little

more challenging. Here, you will test your fear by subjecting yourself to that situation. For example: speak to your friends and purposefully allow yourself to stutter or make a mistake. Or pause awkwardly. See what happens. You'll likely find that the fear is exceptionally overblown compared to the reality. And by experimenting with this, you'll find it's gradually easier to overcome the anxiety. Combine this with management techniques: breathing strategies, meditation, focus, etc., and you will find it becomes easier and easier to overcome the anxiety.

# UNDERSTANDING STRESS, MEDITATION, AND YOUR BRAIN

CHAPTER 07

While meditation is often thought of as being mystical, or somehow connected with religion, the truth is that it is a rigorously studied scientific tool and one that has a profound effect on our biology and the physical structure of our brains.

## YOUR BRAIN ON STRESS VS. MEDITATION

Your brain, when highly stressed, is flooded with cortisol, adrenaline, and acetylcholine. These are what we call 'excitatory neurotransmitters,' which are brain chemicals that get the brain more amped up, and make you feel anxious and alert.

High stress also triggers the many physiological changes we've already seen. But did you know that it will additionally change the way you think? For one, you start to think more negative thoughts and panic more. Your brain works at a higher speed at this point, causing more neurons to fire and more negative possibilities to come to light. At the same time, you'll find that your prefrontal cortex shuts down. It's sometimes referred to as a 'prefrontal lobotomy'! For those who didn't do a neuroscience degree, it means you're losing access to the higher-functioning parts of the human brain that let you plan and think logically. This is why we're prone to making short-term mistakes when we're stressed.

What's more, in a state of heightened arousal such as this, our brain is more likely to lay down new permanent neural connections. This effectively means that we become more likely to repeat the same mistakes and the same thoughts that got us into this state of mind in the first place. For example, do you find yourself constantly worrying about your keys or thinking you've left the oven on? Every time you do this, you reinforce those neural pathways – you effectively reward that behavior and make yourself more likely to worry again the next time. Stress makes it hard to focus on anything, and makes us even more likely to act irrationally. Eventually, this can rewire our brains to a shocking degree.

On the other hand, if you meditate, you'll find that you calm the mind. You enter into slower brainwaves, called alpha and theta. These are accompanied by the production of calming, feel-good neurotransmitters like serotonin, GABA, and even brain-derived neurotrophic factors – this last one can help to improve the formation of new positive networks. This is why those who meditate regularly will find that their brains eventually develop more grey and white matter in the prefrontal cortex: making them more intelligent. The anterior cingulate cortex and other brain regions associated with the 'attentional control network' (executive control network) will grow and thicken also – meaning you can start thinking about more positive and beneficial things. In short, you become smarter, calmer, and more alert. And you gain a skill you can use at any time.

# OPTIMIZING YOUR LIFE, DIET, AND HABITS FOR LESS STRESS AND GREATER FULFILLMENT

CHAPTER 08

Meditation and CBT can get you a long way when it comes to feeling calmer and more fulfilled. But it's not the whole story. If you want to experience a calmer and happier life, then you should also start thinking about the way you live your life, and the things that you focus your efforts on. The great thing about meditation and mindfulness is they will help you to understand just what those important things are – and how to achieve a happier and more content state of mind.

## MINIMALISM

For example, you may wish to start living a more minimal life. We are driven by capitalism and commercialism to try and accrue as much 'stuff' as humanly possible. We do this by buying the things we see in magazines, and by lusting after pictures on Instagram. But the more you spend, the more stress you introduce into your life. The more you have, the more you'll feel you need. And the more you think about the stuff you don't have, the more you'll miss out on the opportunities you have right now.

Ask yourself; do I really need a wide-screen TV? Will it genuinely make my life better, or am I being convinced as such by clever marketing and society? If you don't buy the TV, you will have more money in the bank to provide peace of mind. Moreover, you can spend a little less time sitting in front of it, and a little more time playing outdoors with family, or reading books.

Additionally, you can go through your belongings and think about what you need and what you don't. Throwing out some items will mean less cleaning, less work, and a tidier, calmer environment.

## UNPLUGGING

Speaking of not investing in massive TVs, occasionally unplugging and turning them off is also an excellent way to enjoy a calmer and less stressed life. The very nature of screens – their bright luminescence – means that they trigger a release of the stress hormone cortisol. Not only that, but these portals into other people's lives give us that feeling of dissatisfaction and constantly having to move forward. If you can take some time away from screens and machines, you'll find it's much easier to appreciate what you have already and to find other ways to make fun. If you're currently getting messages from your boss at every time of day, then you should absolutely turn that off!

The act of turning your notifications off is especially important right before bed. So, while it might not be easy to completely do without your phones or other gadgets, you should at least consider having a 'no phone zone' for an hour before you hit the hay. It can make a massive difference to your recovery.

## HEALTH

Exercise, fresh air, nutrition, sleep… all these things are vitally important to you feeling your best. Not only because activity triggers a short-term release of feel-good hormones like serotonin, not only because it feels good to be free from pain and full of energy… but also because being healthy supports long-term calmness. Did you know there are close links between the hormones that regulate our appetite and weight (like thyroid hormones and ghrelin) and those that control our mood?

Think about your health holistically – if you want to perform and feel your best, you need to cleanse yourself inside and out. As your meditation improves, try to gradually remove those things that make you unhealthy, and introduce more positive changes into your life.

# CONCLUSION

# CONCLUSION

And there you have it: at this point, you now have all the knowledge, background, and tools that you need to begin with meditation.

The process doesn't have to be daunting or complex. Just pick the kind of meditation practice that appeals to you most and give it a go! Remember: no pressure to pick this up immediately. Meditation is a journey, and it should be one that you enjoy. Don't try to 'race toward enlightenment.' The real aim is to spend more time being aware of what you're thinking, practicing concentration and focus, and learning to rise above the noise and commotion. It's about understanding you can choose how you react to the world around you – and by doing so, you can enjoy a calmer and more fulfilling life.

Once you've successfully made meditation and mindfulness a big part of your life? What then? Well, you can begin to make your life calmer and simpler in other ways: by cleaning and organizing, by improving your health, and by focusing on the things that matter to you.

Meanwhile, you can practice being mindful during your other activities – and experiment with different types of meditation. Perhaps you might like to join a class such as yoga, or maybe even go on a meditation retreat. The more you progress, the more you'll discover yourself and learn to appreciate the world around you. It's an incredible experience, and you're now ready to take those first rejuvenating steps.

# ABOUT THE AUTHOR

## IAN EVENSTAR

ianevenstar.com
unincorporated.com

Throughout my life I have been a spiritual seeker and was blessed to learn about many of the Eastern philosophies and spiritual practices at a young age – of these disciplines, Zen Buddhism remains the most applicable to my abilities as a creative director and as a designer. Now that I have many years under my belt as a successful designer, agency owner, and Zen practitioner, I have realized that Zen Buddhism was at work this entire time.

The daily practice of its core philosophies is what has helped me become so successful and I want to share that knowledge and guidance with designers everywhere. By connecting the dots between Zen principles and the creative process, I can motivate and empower young generations of designers to get off to the right start, but also help the more experienced designers and creative directors learn to be better at what they do.

www.ingramcontent.com/pod-product-compliance
Lightning Source LLC
Chambersburg PA
CBHW061344040426
42444CB00011B/3081